Disney FAVORITES

ISBN 978-1-5400-8509-2

HAL•LEONARD®

Contact us:
Hal Leonard
7777 West Bluemound Road
Milwaukee, WI 53213
Email: info@halleonard.com

In Europe, contact:
Hal Leonard Europe Limited
42 Wigmore Street
Marylebone, London, W1U 2RN
Email: info@halleonardeurope.com

In Australia, contact:
Hal Leonard Australia Pty. Ltd.
4 Lentara Court
Cheltenham, Victoria, 3192 Australia
Email: info@halleonard.com.au

THE BALLAD OF THE LONESOME COWBOY

from TOY STORY 4

Music and Lyrics by
RANDY NEWMAN

Moderately fast

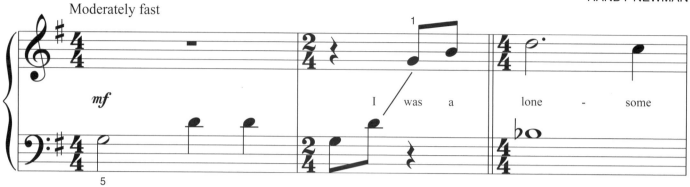

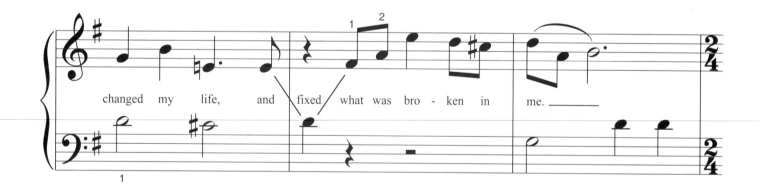

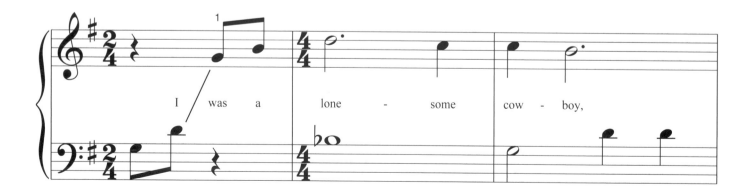

I did-n't have a friend. Now I got friends com- in' out of my ears. I'll

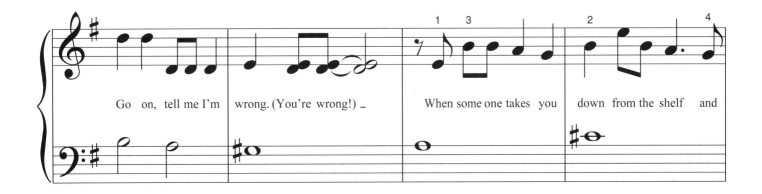

nev- er be lone-some a - gain. ___ You can't be hap-py when you're all by your - self.

Go on, tell me I'm wrong. (You're wrong!) __ When some one takes you down from the shelf and

plays with you some, it's won- der - ful. I was a lone - some

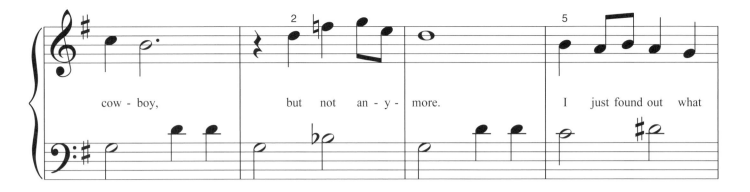

cow - boy, but not an - y - more. I just found out what

love is a - bout. I've nev - er felt this way be - fore. _____

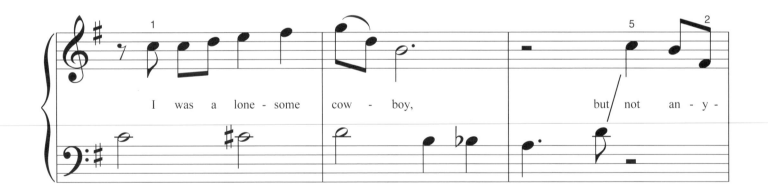

I was a lone - some cow - boy, but not an - y -

more.

SOMETHING WILD

from PETE'S DRAGON

Words and Music by LINDSEY STIRLING,
ANDREW McMAHON, PETER HANNA
and TAYLOR BIRD

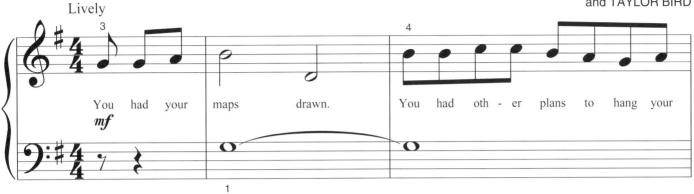

You had your maps drawn. You had oth-er plans to hang your

hopes on. Ev - 'ry road they led you down felt so wrong,

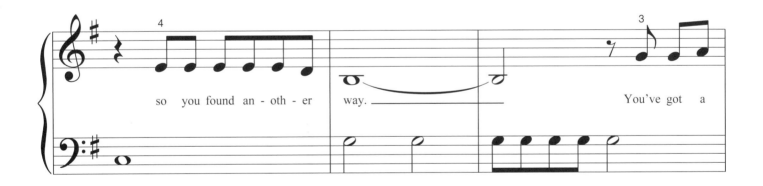

so you found an - oth - er way. ___ You've got a

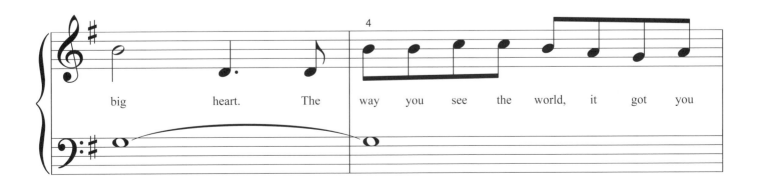

big heart. The way you see the world, it got you

this far. You might have some bruis - es and a few scars,

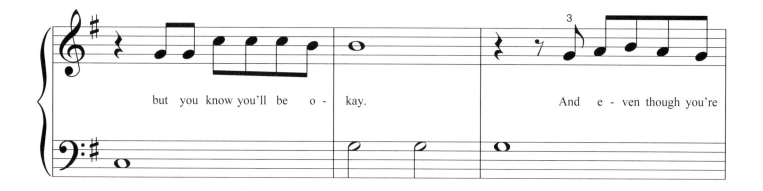

but you know you'll be o - kay. And e - ven though you're

scared, you're strong - er than you know. If you're

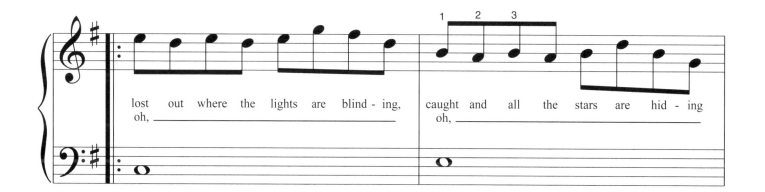

lost out where the lights are blind - ing, caught and all the stars are hid - ing
oh, _____ oh, _____

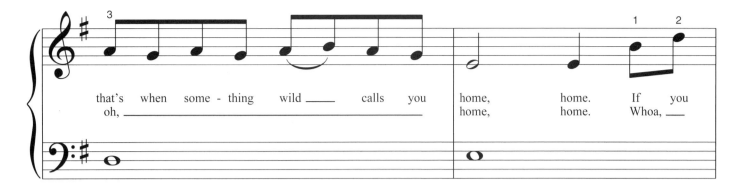

that's when some-thing wild ___ calls you

oh, _____

home, home. If you

home, home. Whoa, ___

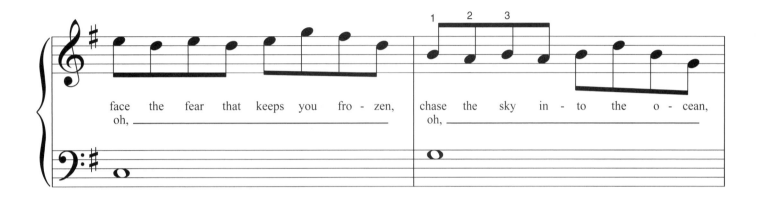

face the fear that keeps you fro-zen,

oh, _____

chase the sky in - to the o - cean,

oh, _____

1.

that's when some - thing wild ___ calls you

oh, _____

home, home. Whoa, ___

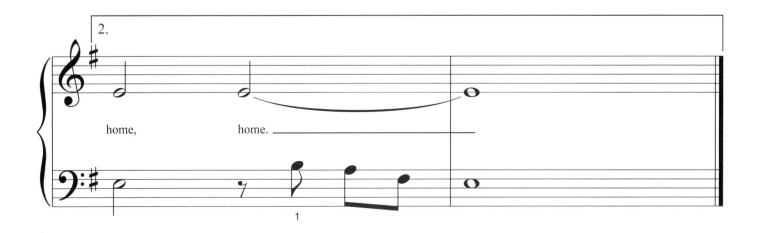

2.

home, home. _____

BUSY DOING NOTHING

from CHRISTOPHER ROBIN

Music and Lyrics by
RICHARD M. SHERMAN

Moderately, with a bounce

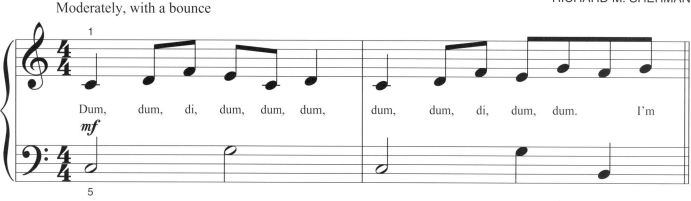

Dum, dum, di, dum, dum, dum, dum, dum, di, dum, dum. I'm

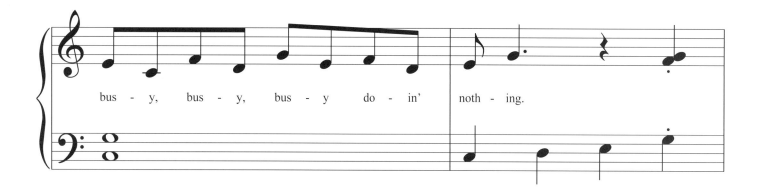

bus-y, bus-y, bus-y do-in' noth-ing.

Do-ing noth-ing, that's the life for me. For

when I'm do-ing noth-ing, I'm bus-y do-ing some-thing,

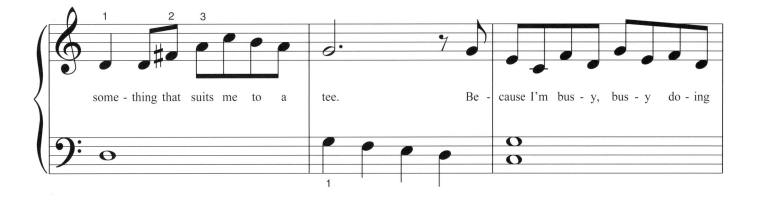

some - thing that suits me to a tee. Be - cause I'm bus - y, bus - y do - ing

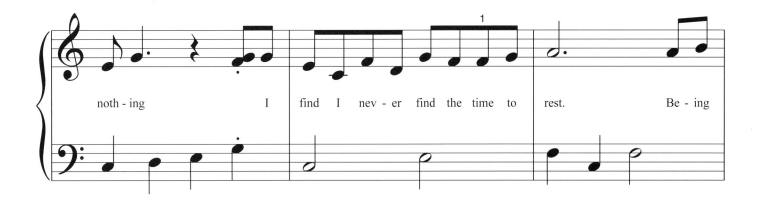

noth - ing I find I nev - er find the time to rest. Be - ing

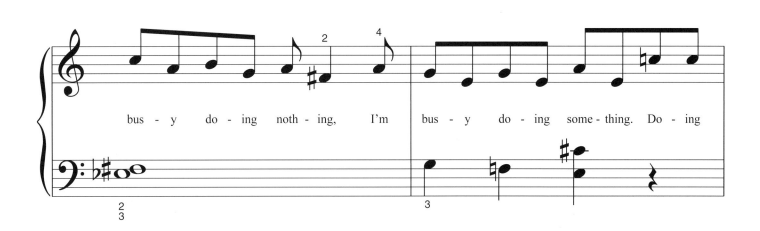

bus - y do - ing noth - ing, I'm bus - y do - ing some - thing. Do - ing

noth - ing is the some - thing I do best.

(UNDERNEATH THE)
LOVELY LONDON SKY

from MARY POPPINS RETURNS

Music by MARC SHAIMAN
Lyrics by SCOTT WITTMAN
and MARC SHAIMAN

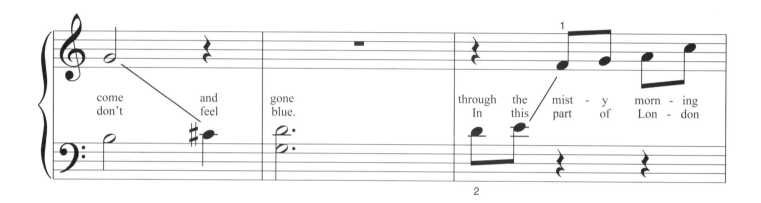

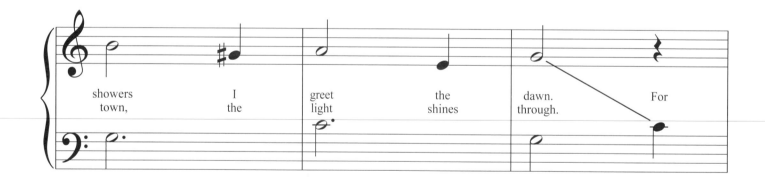

lots of trea - sures to be found,
nev - er know what's up a - head

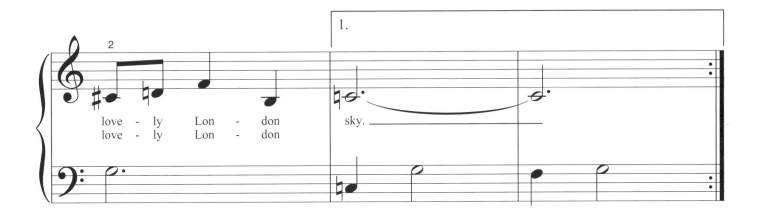

love - ly Lon - don sky. _____
love - ly Lon - don

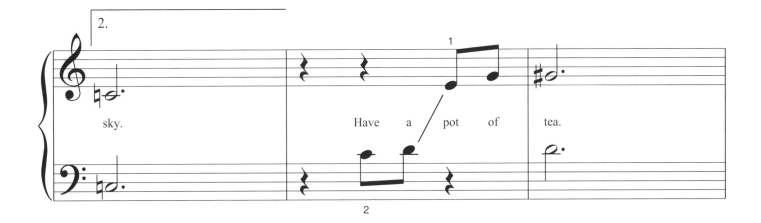

sky. Have a pot of tea.

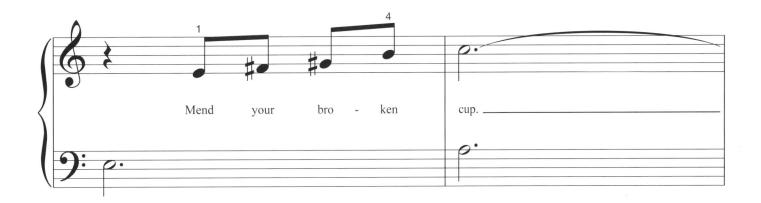

Mend your bro - ken cup. _____

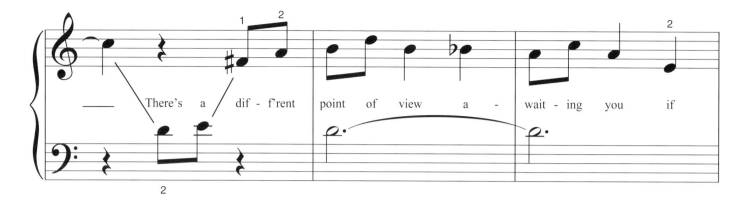

There's a dif - f'rent point of view a - wait - ing you if

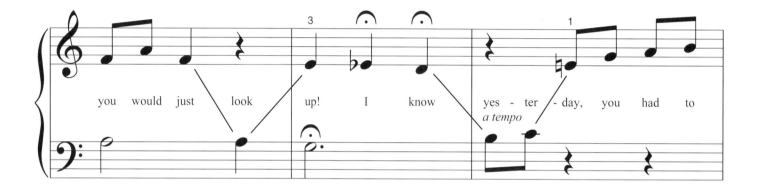

you would just look up! I know yes - ter - day, you had to
a tempo

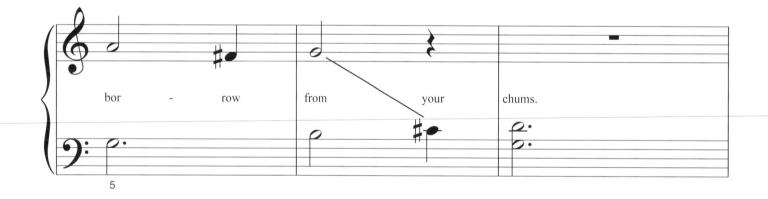

bor - row from your chums.

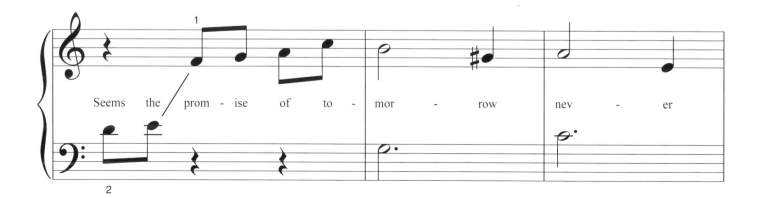

Seems the prom - ise of to - mor - row nev - er

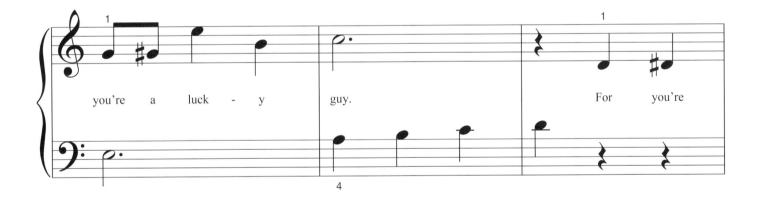

POW! POW! POW! - MR. INCREDIBLES THEME

from INCREDIBLES 2

Music and Lyrics by
MICHAEL GIACCHINO

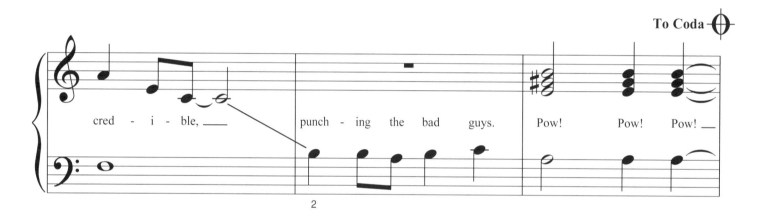

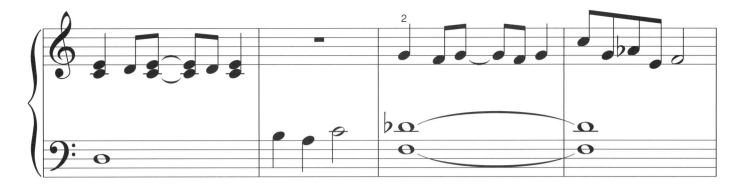

D.C. al Coda

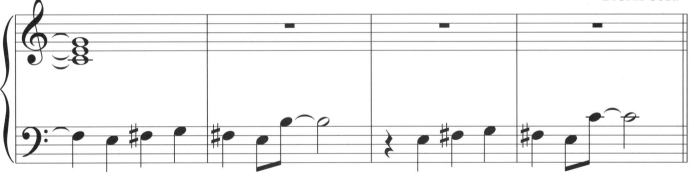

CODA

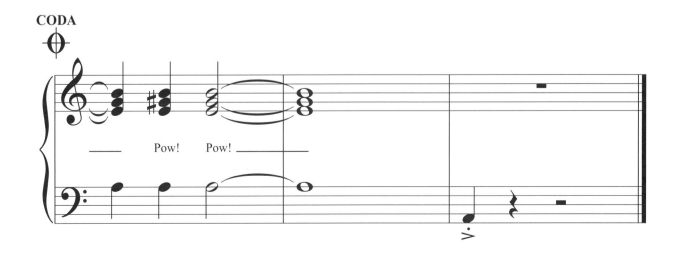

Pow!   Pow!

PROUD CORAZÓN

from COCO

Music by GERMAINE FRANCO
Lyrics by ADRIAN MOLINA

Moderately fast

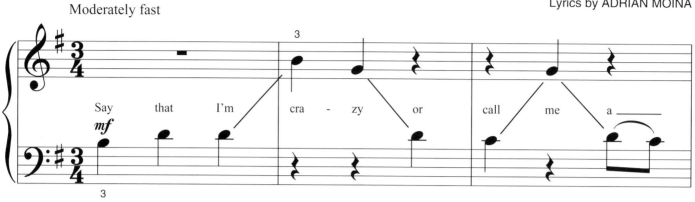

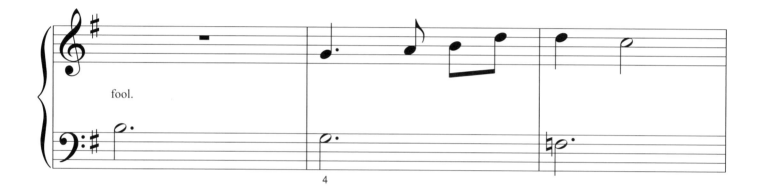

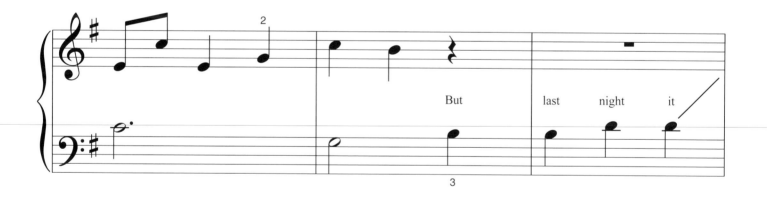

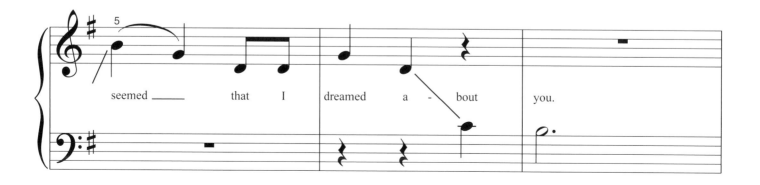

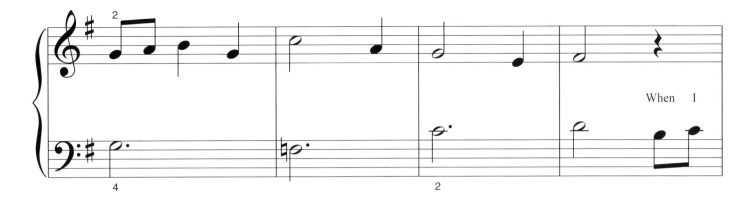

When I

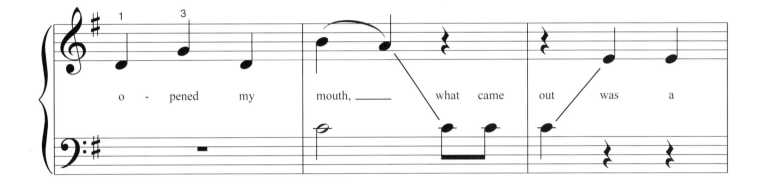

o - pened my mouth, _____ what came out was a

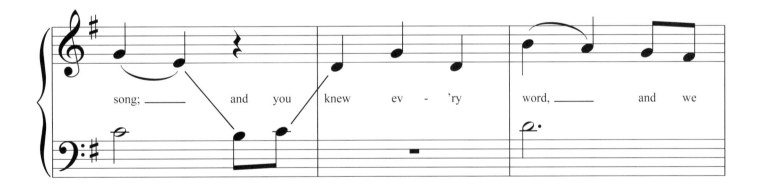

song; _____ and you knew ev - 'ry word, _____ and we

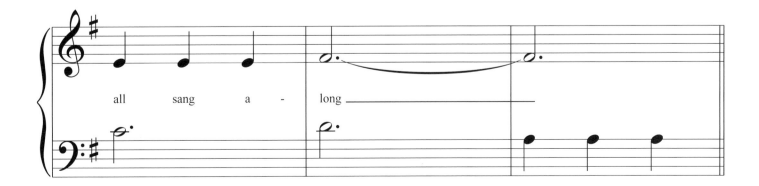

all sang a - long _____

Faster

to a mel - o - dy played _____ on the

strings of our souls _____ and a rhy - thm that

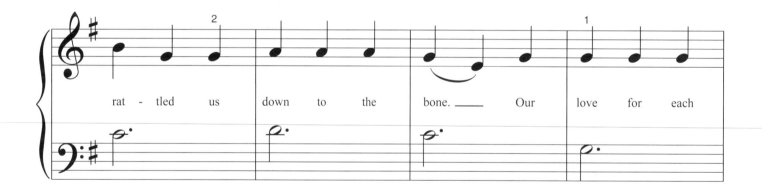

rat - tled us down to the bone. _____ Our love for each

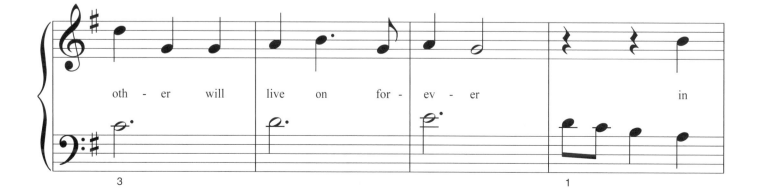

oth - er will live on for - ev - er in

ev - 'ry beat of my proud _____ co - ra - zón. Our

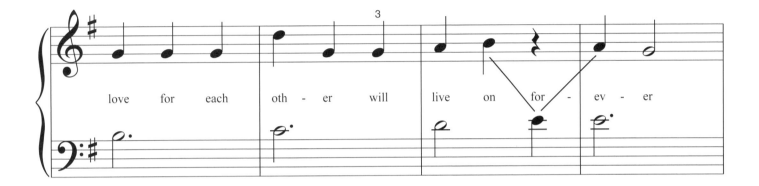

love for each oth - er will live on for - ev - er

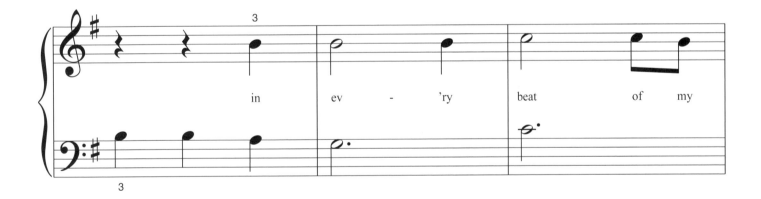

in ev - 'ry beat of my

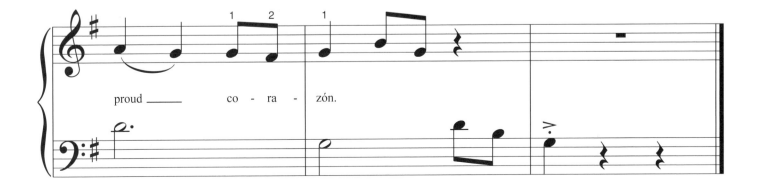

proud _____ co - ra - zón.

SHOW YOURSELF

from FROZEN 2

Music and Lyrics by KRISTEN ANDERSON-LOPEZ
and ROBERT LOPEZ

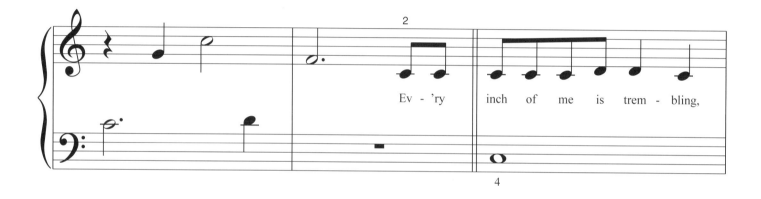

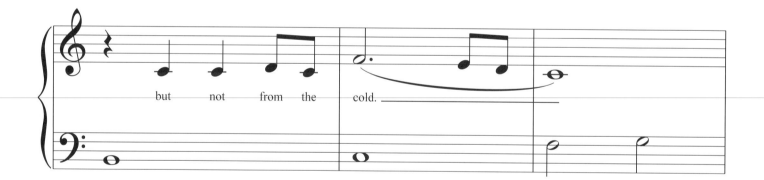

hold.   I can sense you there,   like a friend I've

al - ways known.   I'm ar - riv - ing,

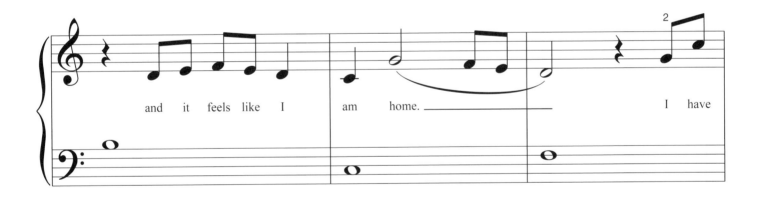

and it feels like I am home.   I have

al - ways been a for - tress, cold se - crets deep in -

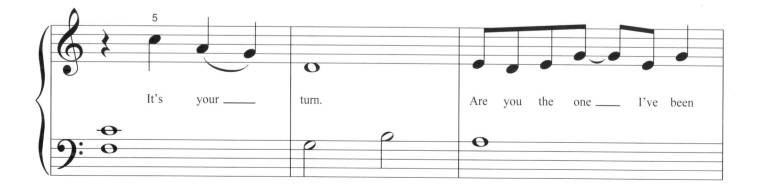

look - ing for all of my _____ life? _____

Show your - self: _____ I'm read - y to learn.

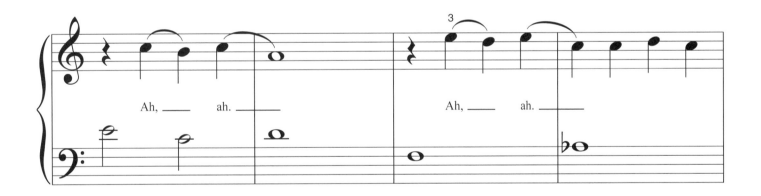

Ah, _____ ah. _____ Ah, _____ ah. _____

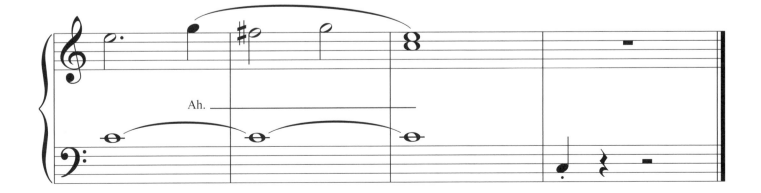

Ah. _____

SPEECHLESS
from ALADDIN (2019)

Music by ALAN MENKEN
Lyrics by BENJ PASEK
and JUSTIN PAUL

Moving along

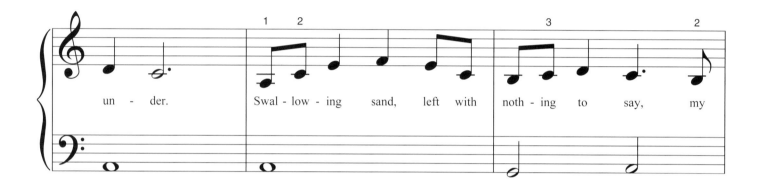

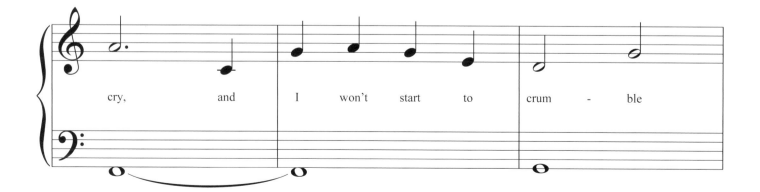

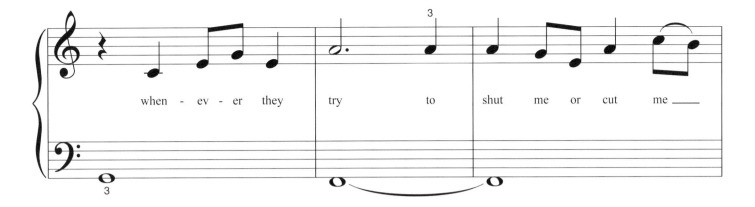

when - ev - er they try to shut me or cut me ____

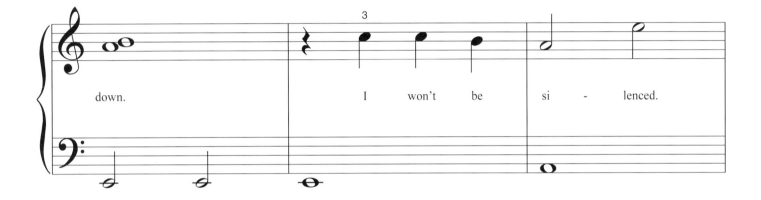

down. I won't be si - lenced.

You can't keep me qui - et. Won't trem - ble when you

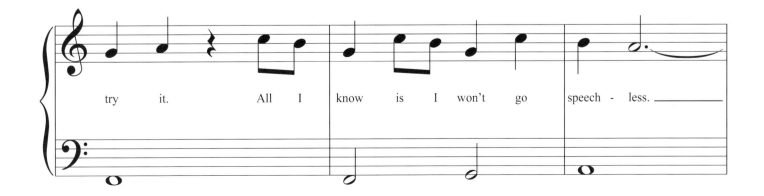

try it. All I know is I won't go speech - less. ____

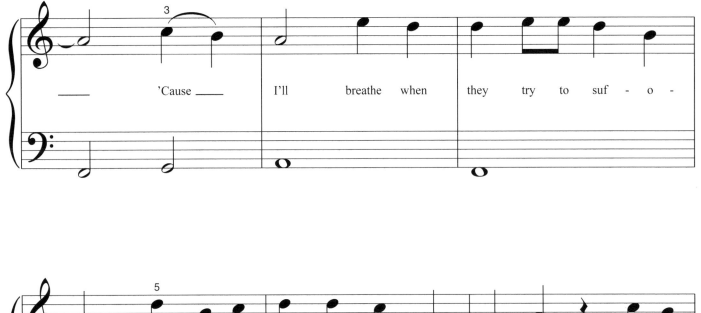

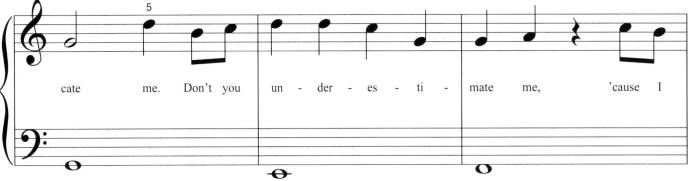

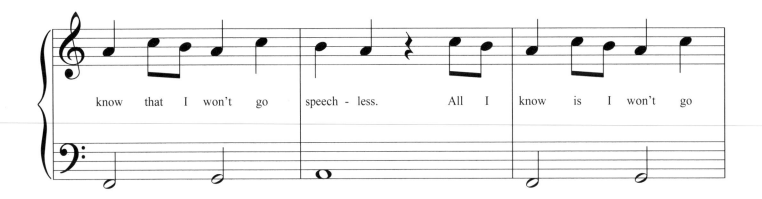

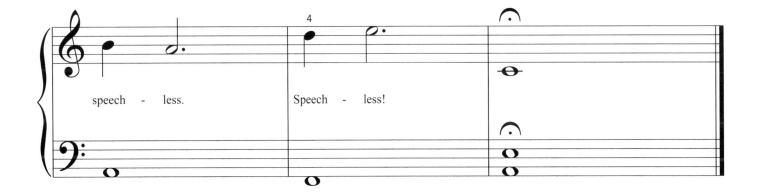

SPIRIT
from THE LION KING (2019)

Written by TIMOTHY McKENZIE,
ILYA SALMANZADEH and BEYONCÉ

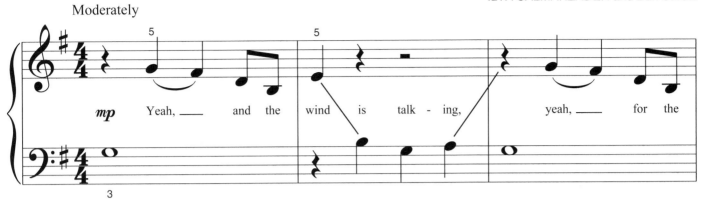

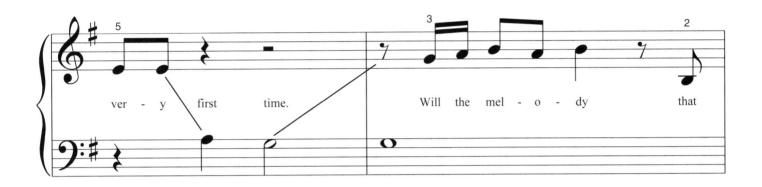

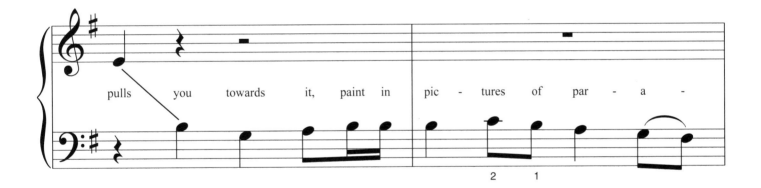

sky, yeah. Watch the light lift your heart up, burn your flame through the

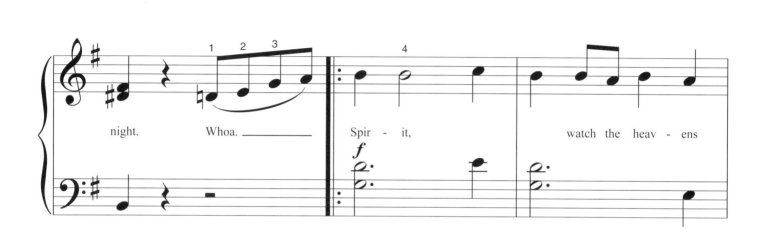

night. Whoa. _____ Spir - it, watch the heav - ens

o - pen, yeah. _____ Spir - it,

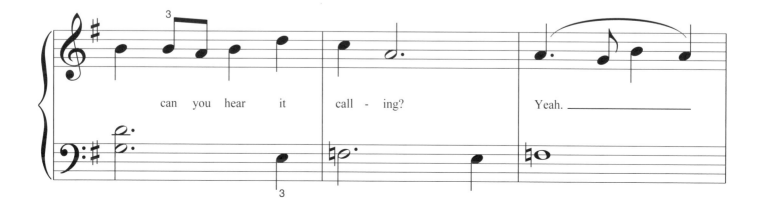

can you hear it call - ing? Yeah. _____

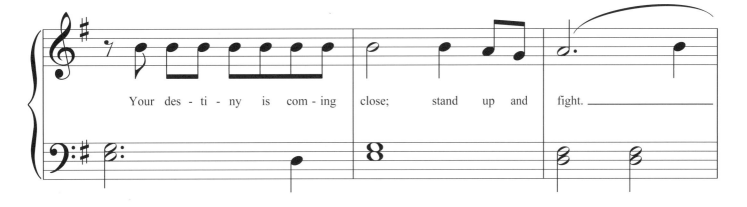

Your des - ti - ny is com - ing close; stand up and fight. _____

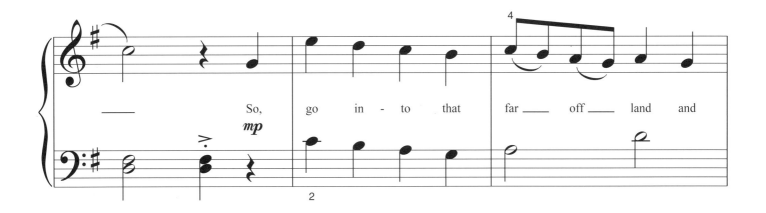

_____ So, go in - to that far ___ off ___ land and

be one with the great I _____ Am, I Am. Boy _____ be -

comes _ a ___ man. Whoa. _____ great I Am. _____

STRONG

from CINDERELLA (2015)

Words and Music by PATRICK DOYLE,
KENNETH BRANAGH and TOMMY DANVERS

Moderately, in 2

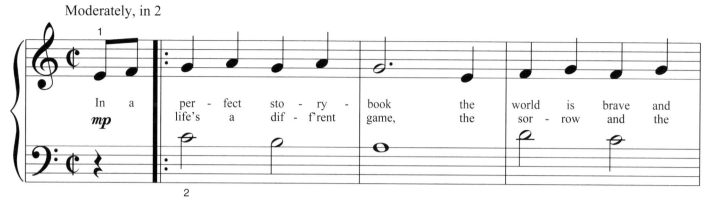

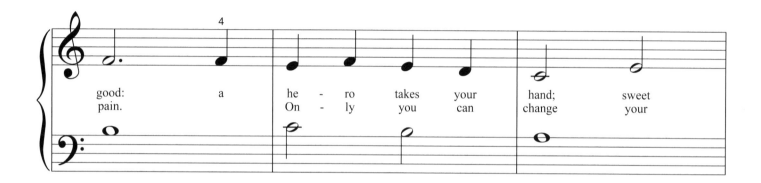

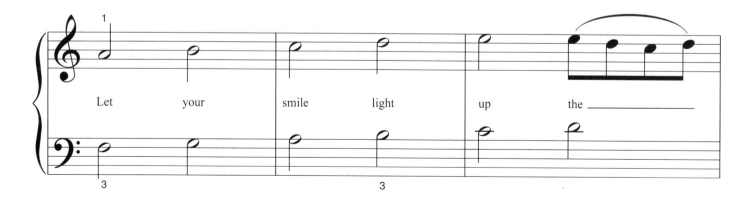

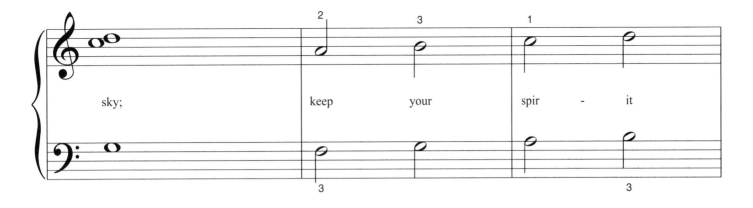

sky; keep your spir - it

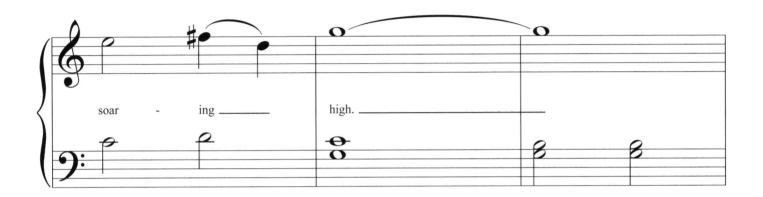

soar - ing _____ high. _____

Trust in your heart, and your soul shines for -

mf

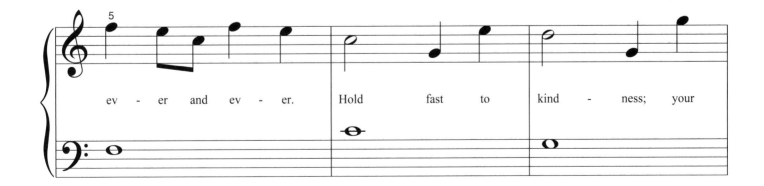

ev - er and ev - er. Hold fast to kind - ness; your

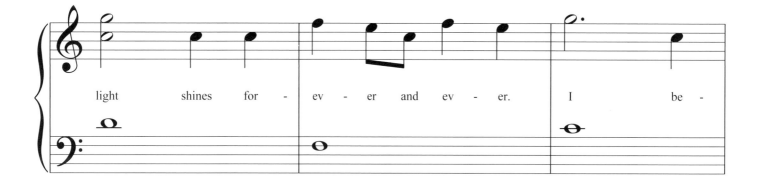

light   shines   for - ev – er and ev - er.   I   be -

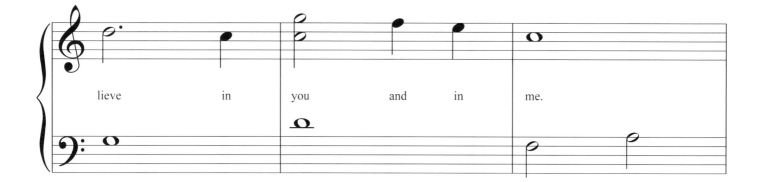

lieve   in   you   and   in   me.

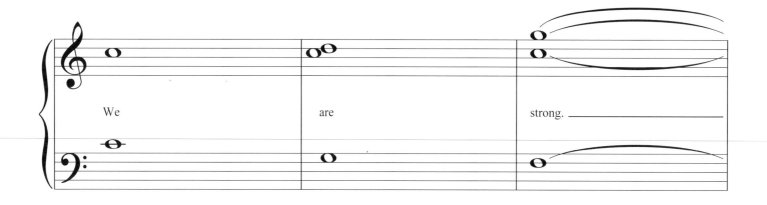

We   are   strong. _____

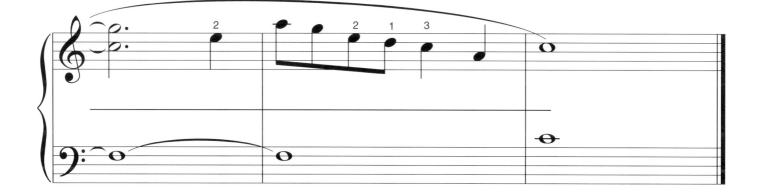